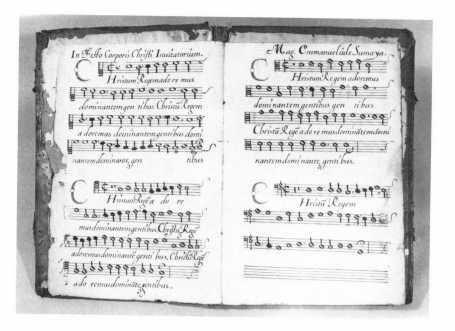

Two
Mexico City
Choirbooks
of 1717

An Anthology of Sacred Polyphony
from the Cathedral of Mexico

Transcription and Commentary
By Steven Barwick

Southern Illinois University Press
Carbondale and Edwardsville

Library of Congress Cataloging in Publication Data
Main entry under title:

Two Mexico City choirbooks of 1717.

    Transcription of the ms. Departamento XXIX, oficina
71, obra 14 in the Mexico City Cathedral and the ms.
Departamento XXIX, oficina 71, obra 24 formerly in the
cathedral, now in the Museo del Virreinato, Tepotzotlán Mexico.
    1. Part-songs, Sacred. I. Barwick, Steven.
II. Catedral de México. Manuscript. Departamento XXIX,
oficina 71, obra. 14. III. Museo Nacional del
Virreinato (Mexico). Manuscript. Departamento XXIX,
oficina 71, obra 24. IV. Title: 2 Mexico City choirbooks of 1717. V. Title: Mexico City choirbooks of
1717.

M2082.T9   82-3047
ISBN 0-8093-1065-1   AACR2

Corrigenda for *Two Mexico City Choirbooks of 1717*

The following facsimiles appear in the text without captions. Facing the title page are *Gloria Patri*, Obra 24, fol. 21v–22 and *Christum Regem*, Obra 24, fol. Ov–1. *Lamentatione Jeremiae, Sabbato Sancto*, Obra 14, fol. 22v–23 appears on p. xxvi. *Alleluia! Dic nobis Maria*, Obra 14, fol. 46v–47 and fol. 49v–50 appears on p. xxvii.

Contents

The Transcription
Part One

Part Two

Preface

When Jesús Bal y Gay published his 1952 edition of
El Códice del Convento del Carmen under the auspices
of the Instituto Nacional de Bellas Artes in Mexico,
he spoke of it as the first volume in a series Tesóro
de la Música Polifónica en México. Although no further
volumes in the series followed directly in Mexico, my
The Franco Codex of the Cathedral of Mexico (Southern
Illinois University Press, 1965) added to the collection; with the present publication, another volume
makes a delayed appearance.

A number of anthologies of music of the colonial
period from various Latin American countries have been
published during the last decade, but only one--Robert
Stevenson's Christmas Music from Baroque Mexico (University of California Press, 1974) deals exclusively
with Mexican sources. Mexico is well represented also,
however, in Stevenson's Latin American Colonial Music
Anthology (General Secretariat, Organization of American States, Washington, D.C., 1975), an admirable
collection including composers who worked in nine OAS
nations. In his preface to Latin American Colonial
Music Anthology, Stevenson provides a summary of the
milestones in the modern publication of Latin American
colonial music; in his Music in Latin America: An
Introduction (Prentice-Hall History of Music series,
1979), Gerard Béhague has further updated this summary.
Currently a multivolume publication of music from
Mexican archives, edited by a number of musicologists
in Mexico, is being sponsored by the Mexican government and is scheduled for an early appearance.

While the music in the Carmen Codex and the Franco
Codex dates from the sixteenth through the middle of
the seventeenth centuries, the repertory in this volume extends into the first quarter of the eighteenth
century and contains works of four composers: Antonio

Rodríguez Mata, Antonio de Salazar, Manuel de Sumaya, and Francisco López Capillas. The edition consists of two parts, each of which is the transcription of a complete choirbook from the archives of the Cathedral of Mexico City. The manuscripts might be considered "companion volumes" inasmuch as both were copied by the same scribe at the cathedral in 1717.

I am grateful to many people for help in preparing this edition. When I was in Mexico in 1947, Señor Jesús Estrada Hernandez showed me for the first time the choirbook containing the López Capillas Magnificats, which I used to some extent in the preparation of my dissertation, "Sacred Vocal Polyphony in Early Colonial Mexico" (Harvard, 1949). For introducing me to the "companion" volume I am indebted to Professor E. Thomas Stanford, who brought it to my attention when he and Dr. Lincoln Spiess were working on their project of cataloguing and microfilming the contents of the musical archives of Cathedrals and other sources in Mexico. This led to their 1969 publication <u>An Introduction to Certain Mexican Musical Archives</u> (Detroit Studies in Music Bibliography-15, Information Coordinators, Inc., Detroit). When their complete catalogue becomes available, the numberings used in the present study can be adjusted to the new index.

For additional valuable assistance in Mexico I am indebted to Professor Roberto Rivera y Rivera and to officials at the Instituto Nacional de Antropología e Historia and the Museo Nacional del Virreinato at Tepotzotlán.

Here at home I owe special thanks to Professor Stanford again for checking the musical text and making valuable suggestions and to Professor Robert Stevenson for giving me his copious notes from the capitular acts of the cathedrals of Mexico and for reading the historical front matter. I would like to express my appreciation also to the Southern Illinois University Office of Research and Projects for financial support for research assistants and travel. My thanks go particularly to Michael Kuhlman for copying the musical text, Roger Davis for additional copy work, to Cathy Hamer for typing the text, and to the other graduate assistants who helped.

Introduction

THE 1717 CHOIRBOOKS

In 1717 the scribe Simon Rodríguez de Guzmán copied
in two choirbooks anthologies of polyphonic choral
works of Antonio Rodríguez Mata (also spelled Matta,
though not in this choirbook), Antonio de Salazar, and
Manuel de Sumaya (commonly spelled Zumaya, though not
in these manuscripts). Both of these volumes were
originally housed in the archives of the Mexico City
Cathedral. The book bearing the Cathedral archive's
inventory numbering Departamento XXIX, Oficina 71,
Obra 14 is still there.1 It contains fifty folios, one
of which is blank, and the numbering begins with folio
nine. The companion volume, containing thirty-eight
folios, is numbered Departamento XXIX, Oficina 71,
Obra 24 and is presently housed in the Museo del
Virreinato at Tepotzotlán, near Mexico City. Another
scribe's copy of settings of the odd-numbered verses
of the Magnificat in each of the eight tones by the
mid-seventeenth century chapelmaster Francisco López
Capillas forms an additional unit with separate pagi-
nation in choirbook Obra 24, adding forty-nine folios
to that volume. This set of Magnificats can also be
found in the manuscript M. 2428 at the Madrid Biblioteca Nacional. The Madrid copy included eight López
Capillas Masses (also found in choirbooks in the
Mexico Cathedral Archives) as well. This copy served
as a handsome presentation volume from Mexico intended
to validate chapelmaster López's right to an ecclesi-
astical benefice.[2] Although this volume contains the
Alleluia of López Capillas, his Magnificats will not
be included here but will remain the subject of another
study.[3]
The two choirbooks resemble each other closely.
Both measure about sixteen by twenty-one inches and

consist of paper leaves bound with boards covered with
brown leather. The books have no illuminations, but
many of the first letters are decoratively drawn. Some
are painted in red or blue, though most are in black.
The scribe's name appears in each book. On the page
before the music begins in Obra 24 an inscription
reads "escrito por Simon Rodríguez de Guzmán año de
1717" (written by S. R. G. in 1717), while the Obra 14
inscription uses an abbreviation: "Guž me escribió año
de 1717" (the book speaking, "Guzmán copied me"). Also
on the page containing Guzmán's signature in Obra 24
one reads in a rather scribbled hand, "cuidado por el
Reverendo Padre Don Angel Moral Collegial de el de los
Infantes de el choro de esta santa yglecia Cathedral
de México el año de 1731" (cared for by the Reverend
Father Don Angel Moral, fellow choirboy of his in this
holy church, the Cathedral of Mexico, 1731). This
would surely indicate that the book was still in use
some fourteen years after it was copied. Inasmuch as
he had been trained in the Cathedral Choir School,
Rodríguez Guzmán was a musician himself. He copied
books of polyphony as well as antiphonaries from 1708
to 1723 and was most likely employed by the Cathedral
as a musician. His copying work may very well have
been one of those "extras" to which the various capitular acts often refer. Another scribe copied the
López Alleluia: Dic nobis Maria (folio 46v-47 through
folio 49v-50) into the last pages of Obra 14. The copy-
ists for the López works are not named.
    Most of the compositions in this edition exemplify
the stile antico of the Baroque era. This manner of
writing--fashioned after Renaissance masters' styles
(sometimes spoken of as stile alla Palestrina) exist-
ing in Europe at this time--was prevalent in Mexico as
far as formal religious music was concerned. Manfred F.
Bukofzer has pointed out that a "mastery of the stile
antico became the indispensable equipment in the composer's education. He was now at liberty to choose in
which style he wanted to write, whether in moderno,
the vehicle of his spontaneous expression, or in
strict antico which he acquired by academic training."[4]
Manuel de Sumaya illustrates this statement clearly,
for he wrote in both styles. Villancicos, making use

of continuo and other instruments (as well as Sumaya's lost opera), show the stile moderno, while his works in this edition demonstrate the stile antico. The latter show what Bukofzer calls "a fictitious strict style which bears the semblance of Renaissance music, but which, in fact is subtly infected with modern licenses."5

An inspection of the works of Maestro Manuel de Sumaya (the Latinized version, Magister Emmanuelis de Sumaya, appears in Obra 24 contained in this collection) shows a sensitive composer with a highly developed contrapuntal technique. An Italianate lyricism is evident in his writing, and his sense of the dramatic punctuates his text settings with impressive silences or colorful chords. In his Lamentations (Sabbato Sancto, Obra 14) for the first nocturn of Holy Saturday matins, for example, he effectively uses the augmented triad on the word lamentatione, while he follows the words cum silentio by rests in all parts. His style is declamatory for the words salutare Dei and dissonant or chaotic for the word holocaustis in his Miserere (folio 42v-43, measure 8). While his sacred style as a whole is the antico, he shows a harmonic sense that is more Baroque than Renaissance when writing in a chordal style. But in his strictly contrapuntal vein he looks back to the Renaissance, adapting the style in a personal way to create an individual result. In the four-part Gloria of his Magnificat III, for instance, he writes a double canon Unitas in Trinitare to exemplify the trinity. The tenor leads while the bass follows at the fifth below and the alto at the fourth above. Above this, the soprano weaves a discant-like melody that gives an ethereal effect: at times it is as far as a twelfth above the other voices. Sumaya used this type of spacing often enough to make it a stylistic characteristic. He handled his melodic lines skillfully, making them serve the expression of the text. The shape of the soprano line on the word lamentatione (Obra 14, folio 22v) clearly depicts a sorrowful wailing and again shows the composer's dramatic sense; in his magnificats and psalms one can see how aptly he makes use of plainsong material.

Of the other works in these volumes, the oldest is
Maestro Antonio Rodríguez Mata's four-voiced setting
of the Lamentations, which bears as title Feria sexta
in Parasceve (for the first lesson in the first nocturn of Good Friday matins). This work, dating from
the first quarter of the seventeenth century, again
represents the stile antico, as does the Alleluia of
Francisco López Capillas. Relating the Easter story
with duet passages in dialogue--one pair of voices
singing "tell us, Mary, what did you see?" and a different pair answering--the piece has a sort of fresh-
ness with a pastorale effect. The Alleluia for all
four voices provides the refrain, which appears several
times in rondo fashion.

The Salazar motet, O Sacrum convivium, contains
Baroque stylistic features not found in the other
pieces. Two four-voiced choirs are treated with brilliance. The use of imitation, antiphonal effects, a
generally rhythmic quality with the use of dotted
rhythms and contrast distinguish this work from the
others in the anthology.

Three of the works appearing in this edition--the
Mata Lamentations, the Salazar O Sacrum Convivium, and
the López Capillas Alleluia--have been recorded by the
Southern Illinois University-Carbondale Collegium
Musicum under the direction of Dr. John Boe and dis-
tributed under the Musical Heritage Society label
MHS 3718 (Renaissance Choral Music from Mexico).

THE CATHEDRAL COMPOSERS

In 1625 the English traveler in the New World,
Thomas Gage, a Dominican, wrote of the religious music
he had heard in Mexico City, declaring the performances
so exquisite that he dared say people were "drawn to
their churches more for the delight of the music than
for any delight in the service of God."[6] It was in
1625 that the earliest music in this book first
appeared. That was the year Antonio Rodríguez Mata
officially became chapelmaster of the Mexico City
Cathedral, although he had been in its musical service
for some time before.[7]

His immediate predecessor was Juan Hernández, who began his association with the cathedral as a singer in 1568. Hernández continued to serve in various capacities--often of a business nature--during the chapelmastership of Hernando Franco (1575-1585), whom he succeeded as chapelmaster on January 17, 1586. Apparently because his interests tended so much in the direction of business affairs he did not develop into the most reliable chapelmaster. The chapter records tell of his delays in delivering new chanzonetas and villancicos for the years 1589 and 1590 and of the chapter's efforts to replace him with a more effective leader. One does not wonder at the chapter's lack of success, however, as even the new archbishop, Juan Pérez de la Serna (1613-1626) seemed unable to dislodge Maestro Hernández. When Antonio Rodríguez Mata appeared before the chapter in September of 1614 with a royal document and the archbishop's endorsement appointing him chapelmaster and half prebend, Hernández was able to stand firm, protesting that he had been the chapelmaster almost thirty years. To placate Hernández and still benefit from the services of Rodríguez Mata, the chapter named Mata Maestro de los infantes del coro (master of the choirboys), a title he spurned the following year for the simpler one of músico in the hopes that Hernández would retire voluntarily in a short time. Hernández, however, managed to stay on in one way or another, and the two musicians continued to exist side by side until 1625 when Mata took over the chapelmastership.

Early in 1620 Hernández, then in his seventies, gave up the office of chapter secretary, a highly-paid post he had held since 1601. Later in the same year, the cathedral musicians as a body submitted a petition to the chapter asking for Hernández's removal, but the chapter refused to honor their request.

While the chapter minutes speak derogatorily of Hernández, they often say good things about Mata. In August of 1618, for example, the chapter awarded him a chaplaincy, and the following year they praised him for his chanzonetas and villancicos, which Hernández no longer composed.

In 1629 Mexico City suffered a disaster that greatly affected the musical life in the Cathedral. Some 27,000 inhabitants were forced to flee from the capital when devastating floods caused tremendous destruction and death. More than 30,000 Indians died in the floods, and, according to reports from Archbishop Manso de Zúñiga to Philip IV, of a previous 20,000 Spanish families, only 400 remained. Consequently the number of musicians on the cathedral payroll was reduced drastically.

The chapter minutes of the 1630s record the progress of recovery from this disaster; funds were allowed for salary increases for a number of the musicians, for new outfits for the choirboys, and for the repair of numerous old choirbooks. Rodríguez Mata became a licenciado in 1639 and two years later a tithe collector--a very lucrative occupation but one that took him away from the cathedral to a territory with headquarters in Toluca. This necessitated the appointment of an interim chapelmaster--Melchor de los Reyes--who had been a cathedral musician since 1632. Mata apparently became a man of some wealth, for he endowed two chaplaincies before he died in 1642.

Luis Coronado and Fabián Ximeno

Rodríguez Mata's successor as chapelmaster at the Mexico City Cathedral was Luis Coronado, who had served as principal organist before his promotion. Although none of Coronado's compositions appear in the 1717 choirbooks, his Passions according to St. Matthew, St. Luke, and St. John appear in the choirbook Departamento XXIX, Oficina 71, Obra 17 of the Cathedral's archives. In addition, his four-part Magnificat can be found in the Cathedral's choirbook Departamento XXIX, Oficina 71, Obra 27.

Coronado was followed by Fabián (Pérez) Ximeno as chapelmaster on March 31, 1648. Like Coronado, Ximeno received his promotion from the post of principal organist of the Cathedral. His reputation extended beyond Mexico City at the time, and, to some extent, he must have been equipped in the area of organ building, for in 1645 he was called to Puebla to repair the

Cathedral organ there. In May of 1648 he again went to Puebla to test the new great organ installed for the consecration of the Puebla Cathedral the following year. No doubt Ximeno was duly impressed with the richer situation in Puebla at the time; musical activities there had gained a splendor and brilliance under the direction of Maestro Juan Gutiérrez de Padilla (chapelmaster, Puebla, 1629-1664) and the supervision of Bishop Palafox y Mendoza. This splendor surpassed the best efforts of Mexico City. The Puebla Cathedral dedication ceremonies of April, 1649, which included choral and instrumental performances of sacred and secular festival music, lasted fourteen days and climaxed a decade of great extravagance.

When Ximeno returned to Mexico City he tried to persuade the chapter to augment his staff and hire more musicians. In 1651 he attempted to lure several of the best instrumentalists from Puebla--a difficult operation, inasmuch as Mexico City would not pay as well as Puebla. One Puebla musician, Nicolás Griñón, supposedly the best harpist in New Sapin, did move to Ximeno's capilla in 1652 at half the salary he had been receiving at Puebla. Ximeno's enticement seemed to entail the offer of more opportunities to earn additional money in Mexico City from extras such as performances at funerals, processions, or receptions. Also, Mexico City may have looked better to Griñón in 1652 when Puebla was surely suffering from a cutback in expenses. Salary cuts, ordered in 1651, reduced Gutiérrez Padilla's pay by 100 pesos, and only three musicians (including Griñón) retained their former salary. In any case, Griñón stayed with the Mexico City Cathedral only seven months, for competitive bands of musicians in the city made it difficult for the cathedral musicians to obtain the "extras" Ximeno had probably promised.

Ximeno, who would have liked more of these "extras" for himself, complained bitterly to the chapter about the situation. He also asked for a salary increase, but the chapter refused to act on either of these counts. In reality, he must have been well off financially, for almost a century after his death in April of 1654 the chapter records made reference to him as one of the two best-paid musicians in cathedral history.

Possibly due to his mid-century contact with the Puebla Cathedral where polychoral works of Gutiérrez de Padilla were being performed, Ximeno developed an interest in this style himself. In the musical archives of the Puebla Cathedral, a Missa de Lorroi (or Lorrio?) provides an interesting example. It is composed for twelve voices and bears the inscription "añadido un coro por el Mo Favián Ximeno" (one choir added by Maestro Favián Ximeno). Also in the Puebla archives are a Magnificat for eight voices, an eight-part Missa de la Batalla, and a four-part motet Spiritus meus attenuabitur. According to Dr. Alice Ray Catalyne, who has seen these works and speaks of them in the second volume (1966) of the Yearbook of the Latin-American Institute for Musical Research, some were labeled simply Maestro Ximeno or Ximenez. Another source of Ximeno's works appears in the set of six small-sized Mexican choirbooks in the collection of the Newberry Library in Chicago.[8] In volume 2 (MS, VM2147, C36, vol. 2) a psalm for three four-part choirs, Beatus vir, and its parody mass for the same combination of voices by Favián Peres Ximeno (as his name appears throughout the manuscripts) can be found. There is also a Magnificat for three choirs and other works. In addition, compositions of Ximeno have been preserved in the Mexico City Cathedral archives in choirbook Departamento XXIX, Oficina 71, Obra 27, which contains two five-part psalms--Quia inclinavit and Confitebor.[9]

Francisco López Capillas

Bachiller Francisco López Capillas was hired the month Ximeno died to serve as both chapelmaster and principal organist in the Mexico City Cathedral. His annual salary was 500 pesos. Born in Mexico City[10] about 1612, he had such a fine reputation in Mexico by the middle of the seventeenth century that the chapter commissioned him to compose the Corpus Christi, Assumption and Saints Peter and Paul chanzonetas on the very date they announced the opening for the chapelmaster

position. While the chapter allotted forty days for
applications to come in, they hired López Capillas on
the tenth day. Obviously the cathedral chapter already
knew López's work through a choirbook he presented to
them on March 10, 1654, about a month before Ximeno's
death.

As his assistant he was assigned Francisco Vidal,
Ximeno's nephew, who had already been serving as organ
builder and tuner. Vidal alternated with him every
other week as conductor-organist, except at double
feasts. At the more solemn feasts, López was to direct
while Vidal played. The less fortunate Juan Coronado,
who had been selected as Ximeno's assistant in 1648,
was retained as a less important helper as well.

In 1656, the year of the first solemn dedication of
the Cathedral of Mexico City, López Capillas was
called upon for some extraordinary music. The viceroy,
the Duke of Alburquerque, was highly impressed with
López Capillas's abilities and proposed a special musical event for St. James (July 25) when four bishops
were to be consecrated. For this occasion López Capillas composed a gigantic polychoral work. He wrote four
different masses--each complete in itself--which were
given to different choirs in the city for rehearsal
under their own chapelmasters. Later, for the consecration ceremonies the four masses were sung simulta-
neously in the Cathedral. The polychoral tradition,
which existed in Puebla and had been continued in
Mexico City by Ximeno, reached a high point in this
work of López, who won the complete confidence of the
new archbishop before the year was finished.

Works of López have been preserved principally in
choirbooks associated with the Mexico City Cathedral.
As stated in the preface, his eight six-verse settings
of the Magnificat for four parts appear in a supple-
mental volume bound with the book copied by Guzmán
in 1717. Still in the Cathedral's archives are two
other choirbooks of López's works alone. One of these
may be the volume of his works he presented to the
Cathedral in 1654. The choirbook _Inventario: Departamento XXIX, Oficina 71, Obra 25_ contains three parody
masses--each with its own parodied work--Re _Sol_ (four
parts) on a six-part _canción_ by Riscos, _Aufer a nobis_

(four parts) after his own motet, and Super alleluia
(five parts), also on his own short four-part Alleluia. Following this is another Alleluia: Dic nobis
Maria (four parts), an Easter outburst and the same
piece which was copied into Choirbook Obra 14 by
another hand. The presence of this work, as well as
the Magnificats bound with Obra 24, testifies to the
popularity that López's music was still enjoying during the first quarter of the eighteenth century.

Joseph de Agurto y Loaysa

López died on January 18, 1674, at Mexico City, and
Agurto y Loaysa (or de Loaysa y Agurto, as his name
appears on title pages of villancicos published in
Mexico City in 1685 and 1686) succeeded López as maestro de los villancicos in 1676. Later in the same year
his title became maestro compositor. These titles
appear on publications of villancicos by Sor Juana de
la Cruz. The title pages indicate that the music for
the villancicos was provided by Loaysa, but the published books contain the poetry only. Whether Loaysa
was actually replacing López at this time or whether
the new villancico composer was only appointed to do
that composing from which López had tried to escape
some twelve years earlier may be clarified in the
future, but we know that Loaysa did become the chapelmaster eventually, for his name appears as maestro de
capilla on an undated publication of Sor Juana. Some
of his villancicos have survived in the Jesús Sánchez
Garza Collection at the Instituto de Bellas Artes in
Mexico City and in the Mexico City Cathedral's Choirbook Inventario: Departamento XXIX, Oficina 71, Obra 15
his name appears on folio 46v containing a four-part
hymn, Sanctissimi Josephi. Other unidentified motets,
hymns, or psalms in this volume may also be by Loaysa.
He was a chapelmaster who had little patience with the
choir, and the chapter minutes of 1681 speak of cutting
the number of choirboys to twenty, a proposal of the
archdeacon which Loaysa supported. In 1684 he was con-
tent to turn the soprano lead over to the castrato
Bernado Melendes (or Melanges ?) who had sung in the
Puebla Cathedral before moving to Mexico City.

Loaysa's death date is not known at present, but his chapelmastership ended a few years after this time.

Antonio de Salazar

Antonio de Salazar became the chapelmaster of the Cathedral at Mexico City on September 3, 1688. Born in Spain about 1650, he was a prebendary in Seville before going to Mexico. He was appointed chapelmaster of the Cathedral of Puebla July 11, 1679, where he remained until just a few days before moving to the capital. During his nine years at Puebla he established a fine reputation for his versatility and productivity. Surviving in the Puebla Cathedral archives are such representative compositions as six Latin hymns (motet-type settings) in Libro de Coro V, a Magnificat (even verses for five voices), Oficio de Defuntos (first nocturn, four voices), and a Salve Regina for eight voices. His name also appears on the title pages of four villancico cycles by Sor Juana, which were published and performed in Puebla.

Salazar's appointment at Mexico City came after winning a publicly announced competition set up by nineteen chapter members. In addition to tests in plain chant and counterpoint, the five competing candidates had to set the texts of a Latin motet and a Spanish villancico within a day. The compositions were performed a few days later, and Salazar received eight votes, while his nearest contender got only three. His salary was set at 500 pesos yearly plus extras, including copying assistance and sufficient music paper for all his compositions. He was also given the understanding that his works would be preserved in the archives, as was the practice at Puebla.

Upon accepting the appointment, Salazar at once took stock of what was actually in the Cathedral's musical archive and found that the books of polyphonic music in particular were missing. When they were recovered from one of the musicians who had taken them home (a maestro Carrión), costly repairs were needed before they could be properly and safely stored in a new and separate archive for which only Salazar had the key. In Mexico City Salazar continued to be as

productive as he had been at Puebla. He set entire
villancico cycles by Sor Juana de la Cruz in 1690,
1691, and 1692. In 1701 and 1702 certain cathedral
ceremonies included his Te Deum. His four-voiced
hymns--Egregie Doctor, Christe sanctorum, and Miris
Modi, preserved in the Cathedral's choirbook Inventario: Departamento XXIX, Oficino 71, Obra 15--con-
sist of two sections. For each, the first part is by
Salazar and the second part by his pupil, Manuel de
Sumaya. Both parts of the four-voiced Vexilla Regis,
found in the same book, are by Salazar, however.

During the last decade of the seventeenth century
the Mexico City Cathedral acquired a new great organ
which was built in Madrid by Jorge de Sesma. The
Cathedral chantre spent several months in Spain (1689-
90) supervising the initial work on the organ and
arranging for its installation in Mexico. Not until
October, 1692, did the builders bring the organ to
Mexico, however, and then an additional two years were
required before completion of the organ case and other
parts not built in Spain. One-third of the contracted
price of 12,000 pesos was still due in October of 1694,
but the chapter insisted upon inspection and approval
by Joseph de Ydiáquez, principal organist since 1673,
Francisco de Orsuchil, second organist and tuner since
1656, and Dr. Juan de Narváez, a prebendary, and two
other Cathedral musicians before making the final set-
tlement. Eventually the chapter decided to pay an
additional amount for some modifications to improve
the instrument and correct unsatisfactory features,
which the inspection committee reported in May of 1695.
With the new great organ installed, the chapter no
doubt realized the importance of training more organ-
ists. Salazar helped develop a sort of scholarship pro-
gram that would prepare the next generation of church
musicians.

Salazar and Ydiáquez together produced outstanding
pupils. One choirboy, Cristóbal Antonio de Soña, took
daily lessons from Ydiáquez. In January of 1693 the
chapter gave him a twenty-peso yearly salary to help
clothe him but added the stipulation that he would be
fined for each lesson he missed. In May, 1694, the
dean recommended that the choirboy Manuel de Sumaya be

allowed thirty pesos for clothing and a yearly salary
of fifty or sixty pesos while studying with Ydiáquez
and assisting in Cathedral services when required.
Another youth, Juan Téllez Xirón, started with a yearly
eighty-peso salary in January, 1697, while studying
organ with Ydiáquez.

Salazar also took pupils supported by the chapter.
One very talented choirboy, José Pérez de Guzmán,
began studying with him in January, 1696. He was given
a fifty-peso salary, and in 1708 he left the Cathedral
to become the chapelmaster at Oaxaca. At this time the
chapter decided to insist that all three cathedral
organists--Sumaya, Téllez, and Esquivel--teach talented
choirboys polyphony, so that there would continue to
be new candidates for important positions. Another
notable pupil was the bachiller Manuel Francisco de
Cárdenas from Guadalajara who had taken a four-month
leave in July, 1700, to prepare for sochantre (sub-
chanter) with Salazar. He had a very fine voice and
was invited to remain at Mexico City, where in 1710 he
was earning 200 pesos from the Cathedral while contin-
uing to study at Salazar's house.

On January 10, 1710, Salazar petitioned the chapter
to excuse him from his duties of teaching the choirboys. He stated that not all needed to study counter-
point--a subject he would be happy to continue teaching at his home to prospective choral leaders neverthe-
less. At the time of this request he was sixty years
old, almost blind, and in bad health; and so the chapter agreed to release him from his teaching duties at
the choirschool, although they did not want to discon-
tinue the counterpoint instruction. His infirmities
kept him at home more and more so that a formal substitute had to be engaged. Salazar died in 1715.

Manuel de Sumaya

Manuel de Sumaya (commonly spelled Zumaya) was asked
to teach counterpoint in Salazar's place in the choirschool. In addition, he was selected to substitute for
Salazar in the Cathedral. He became acting chapelmaster in 1711, and in 1715 he was appointed to the full
post after successfully passing public tests of his

ability. Bachiller Francisco de Atienza, who had substituted for Salazar many times seven years earlier
(perhaps during an earlier illness of Salazar), was
older than Sumaya and tried to win the appointment on
this basis. The chapter voted in favor of Sumaya, however, and Atienza moved to Puebla to fill the vacancy
created by the death of Maestro Miguel de Dallo y Lana,
who had succeeded Salazar there when he left for
Mexico City in 1688.

Sumaya was born in Mexico City. He received his
early musical training as a choirboy in the Cathedral,
displaying an outstanding talent that quickly won the
notice of the dean and the chapter. Performing as a
seise (one of six choirboys in some cathedrals, who
sing and dance in certain festivals) until May 24,
1694, he then asked to be dismissed from the Cathedral
employ with the customary terminal pay granted gradu-
ating seises. He petitioned for funds to study organ
at this time, and, as stated above, he was awarded a
grant, for the dean did not want to see a boy with so
much musical talent become a friar. The dean also felt
that the cathedral authorities had an obligation to
train candidates for their own offices. With his clothing allotment and yearly salary of fifty or sixty
pesos he also received daily organ lessons with
Ydiáquez and studied (presumably composition) with
Maestro Antonio Salazar. At the same time he completed
his training for the priesthood, and by an act dated
February 12, 1700, he was given a dispensation from
the normal intervals between tonsure and the orders.
He was made Cathedral organist about this time; he
also cultivated linguistic and literary interests,
acquired a fluency in Italian, and in 1708, published
an original play, El Rodrigo.

In January, 1711, a new viceroy, the Duke of
Linares, Don Fernando de Alencastre Noroña y Silva,
arrived in Mexico City and without delay made use of
Sumaya's talents. A devotee of Italian opera, the duke
commissioned Sumaya to translate Italian libretti and
to write new music for them. He was highly satisfied
with the composer's work. On the first of May, 1711,
Sumaya's opera, La Parténope, was produced, at the
duke's order, in the viceregal palace to celebrate the

saint's day of Philip V. Only the libretto survives, in a printed bilingual edition of Italian and Spanish (in the Biblioteca Nacional in Mexico City), but it has been assumed that the music was Italian in style, which would have pleased the duke. The roles of leading ladies may have been sung by cathedral choirboys, although the choir had used a castrato as early as 1684. This opera was significant historically, for it was the first opera in Mexico, and, as far as is known, it remains the first opera produced in North America.

Sumaya's apparent facility with the Italian style and language raises some questions that cannot be answered at this time. Some historians have postulated that he studied or lived in Italy during his youth. The libretto to La Parténope was by Silvio Stampiglia, and an earlier opera by the obscure Luigi Manzo using the same libretto had been produced in Naples in 1699. It has been suggested, then, that unless Sumaya had lived in Italy, or more particularly in Naples, it would have been difficult for him to have become acquainted with the libretto. Still, it is possible that the new duke brought to Mexico this and many other Italian libretti which he gave to Sumaya for translation and musical setting. From what is presently known of Sumaya's activities around the beginning of the eighteenth century, however, it is easy to see how he could have spent some time abroad--conceivably after he became a priest. Perhaps the reason Atienza substituted frequently for Salazar in 1703 was that Sumaya, in fact, was not in Mexico City at that time and hence could not be called upon for such substitution work.

The 1717 choirbooks of this edition represent the chapelmaster at the height of his term of office. Manuscripts containing his religious music have been preserved in Puebla, Oaxaca, and as far away as Guatemala City, as well as in private collections. A very versatile composer, Sumaya wrote not only polyphonic church music, but also villancicos calling for continuo and ensemble accompaniment, which were tantamount to short solo cantatas. The 1717 books were in use in 1731, as mentioned above, according to an inscription by their "caretaker," Father Don Angel Moral, on a blank page

at the beginning of <u>Obra</u> <u>24</u>. About this time, however,
some changes in the choir situation are noted in the
capitular acts. For example, five boy choristers were
dismissed for ineptness in 1731, while a year later
the master of the choirboys, <u>bachiller</u> Juan Peres, was
taken to task for neglecting to teach plainsong. By
the end of 1733 the choirschool was suspended, over
Sumaya's protest, and by 1734 plans for the construc-
tion of two matching great organs were under way. By
1736 more emphasis was being placed on instrumental
music. The new organs pleased the archbishop-viceroy
very much, and many new instrumentalists were hired
that year. The choir was cut down markedly the following year by the plague, and on September 5, 1736, the
long-time dean of the Cathedral, Tomás Montaño, left
for his new post as bishop of Oaxaca.

Shortly after (in 1739), Sumaya followed Montaño to
serve as chaplain--a move that stunned the Cathedral
chapter. They tried to get him to return by sending
formal letters declaring that he had accepted Bishop
Montaño's invitation to Oaxaca without Mexico City
Cathedral license. By January, 1740, Sumaya still had
not answered the letters, and so the chapter sent a
final admonition via courier. To make matters worse,
Sumaya had taken with him the book recording the
amounts due the various musicians for all "extra ceremonies." Not until September did the chapter formally
begin the search for another chapelmaster, but no
suitable candidate presented himself for audition.

In October, 1742, Bishop Montaño died, and Sumaya
became a <u>cura</u> <u>interino</u> <u>del</u> <u>sagrario</u> (interim curate).
Mexico City tried again in January, 1743, to get
Sumaya to return, for they thought his tentative position in Oaxaca would no longer hold him there. Sumaya,
however, stayed in the southern city where, after giving up his temporary post to another candidate, he
became the chapelmaster of the Cathedral on January 11,
1745, following <u>Maestro</u> Tomás Salgado. During the next
nine years the musical life of Oaxaca developed under
Sumaya's leadership to the highest point recorded in
its history. In addition to his work as musical direc-
tor and priest in Oaxaca, Sumaya continued to pursue
his literary interests, translating from Italian into

Spanish a biography of a Jesuit scholar, Sertorio Caputo (Caputi) (1566-1608). He died in Oaxaca in 1754.

In The New Grove Dictionary of Music and Musicians (Macmillan, 1980), volume 20, p. 715, Alic Ray Catalyne has summarized Sumaya's accomplishments as follows:

> Zumaya's career encompassed a time of changing tastes, as is borne out by the larger number of string than wind players at the cathedral, and by his own villancico-cantatas, with their florid Italianate arias, continuo recitatives, graceful figuration for violins and richly coloured harmonic vocabulary. In his Latin works, however, Zumaya retained the decorum and the traditional polyphonic treatment that characterized Spanish cathedral music. Zumaya was the earliest known opera composer on the North American continent . . . and (with the loss of Salazar's four villancico cycles of 1690-97) the composer of the earliest extant music glorifying the Mexican Virgin of Guadalupe.

FACSIMILIES

EDITORIAL POLICIES

In preparing a transcription intended for practical performance as well as for scholarly use, I have followed procedures that show the music as it appeared in the original sources. Both choirbooks were written entirely in the conventional white mensural notation of the late sixteenth century, and for this edition all of the note values have been reduced by one-half. The music has been transcribed from the choirbook format (soprano and alto parts in the upper portions of the book and tenor and bass parts in the lower) into score at the original pitch level. In the two-choir piece by Salazar, Choir I appears on the verso side of the folio and Choir II on the other side. The voices are aligned for each choir with the soprano at the top of the page and alto, tenor, and bass beneath. The original clefs and time and key signatures are provided at the beginning of each composition, but no incipits are given because of the consistency of the reduction. For the transcription, modern clefs--treble for soprano and alto, tenor (transposed treble) for tenor, and bass clef for the bass part--have been used.

In both choirbooks accidentals appear in various manners. A flat or a sharp sign may appear immediately before a note (in which case it appears in this location in the transcription) or an accidental, written in another hand, may be found either below or above a note in a passage. The use of the accidental in this manner would seem to record the practice at the time the music was being performed. In the transcription, I have placed accidentals of this type above the notes in question as ordinary musica ficta indications. Musica ficta indications that are mine alone have been placed in parentheses above the notes to be altered. Sharp signs that are used to cancel flats in the manuscript have been changed to natural signs. In making musica ficta suggestions of my own, I have tried to apply the rules of mi contra fa and subsemitonium modi as well as practices that might seem to be indicated by added directives found in the manuscripts themselves.

I have placed texts under the notes as they appear
in the sources and have enclosed editorial text exten-
sions in brackets. I have adhered to the orthography
of the Liber Usualis but have not repositioned the
underlay. I have italicized bass line words in the two
Sumaya Misereres, in the Salazar O Sacrum Convivium
and in parts of the López Capillas Alleluia to show
places where a text was lacking. This text omission
probably indicated an instrumental use at the time.

Ligatures are indicated throughout the edition by
semibrackets (⌐ ¬), and blackened notes or coloration
are enclosed in parentheses.

For actual performance, in addition to a possible
use of instruments, some changes in text placement
could be desirable, and some use of transposition
might improve the effect as well. It would be expected,
also, that performers today might want to make further
editorial changes in the application of musica ficta,
for one cannot know when the additional indications
found in the manuscripts appeared or whether they
necessarily had the approval of the composers.

NOTES

The following abbreviations are used in references to
the musical text: sop (soprano) or sop I or II (soprano
I or II), alt (alto), ten (tenor), ba (bass), m. (mes-
sure), L (longa), B (brevis), S (semibrevis), M (mini-
ma), Sm (semiminima) and ms (manuscript). The transla-
tions are from The Roman Breviary (New York: Benziger
Brothers, 1964) and Franciscan Daily Missal and Hymnal
(Patterson, NJ: St. Anthony Guild Press, 1967).

Adjuva nos Deus (Sumaya), folio 0v-1
This piece is a five-voice setting of the ninth verse
of Vulgate Psalm 78. Sung at Friday matins, the
psalm's antiphon has a text that paraphrases the ninth
verse. The motet, however, was probably used at Mass
and other religious events. Anthony M. Cummings in his
article "Toward an Interpretation of the Sixteenth-
Century Motet," Journal of the American Musicological
Society 34 (1981), 59, pointed out that in the six-

teenth century the motet employed liturgical texts or
combinations of them, but because of the use of com-
plex polyphonic procedures inappropriate to some
liturgical contexts and other features, the motet in
the sixteenth century should be defined as "a para-
liturgical compositional type." Probably the same
would hold true for the time this motet was performed.

Text

Adjuva nos, Deus salutaris noster; et propter gloriam
nominis tui Domine, libera nos et propitius esto pec-
catis nostris propter nomen tuum.

Help us, O God our savior,
because of the glory of your name;
deliver us and pardon our sins
for your name's sake.

Corrections

m. 9, ba, ms has

m. 11, ba, ms has an <u>F</u>

m. 12, sop I and alt both in ms are

m. 14, ba, ms has <u>B</u>

m. 21, sop II, ms has

m. 29, ten, ms has

m. 66, sop II, ms has

<u>Miserere mei Deus secundum</u> (Sumaya), folio 4v-5
This is a four-voiced setting of the odd numbered
verses and the second half of verse 20 of Psalm 50.
Given with the title in the manuscript is the date
"año 1717," which distinguishes it from the other
<u>Miserere</u> by Sumaya in this volume. In a margin in a
hand other than the copyist's one reads "para los
viernes" (for Fridays). Sung at Lauds in Holy Week,

Psalm 50 was also used in the Office for the Dead and for the burial service. The setting is in a simple chordal style for an <u>alternatim</u> performance.

Text

1. Miserere mei, Deus, secundum magnam misericordiam tuam.

   Have mercy on me, O God, in your goodness.

3. Amplius lava me ab iniquitate mea: et a peccato meo munda me.

   Thoroughly wash my guilt from me and of my sin cleanse me.

5. Tibi soli peccavi, et malum coram te feci: ut justificeris in sermonibus tuis, et vincas cum judicaris.

   Against you only have I sinned and done what is evil in your sight--that you may be justified in your sentence, vindicated when you condemn.

7. Ecce enim veritatem dilexisti: incerta et occulta sapientiae tuae manifestasti mihi.

   Behold, you are pleased with sincerity of heart, and in my inmost being you teach me wisdom.

9. Auditui meo dabis gaudium et laetitiam: et exsultabunt ossa humiliata.

   Let me hear the sounds of joy and gladness; the bones you have crushed shall rejoice.

11. Cor mundum crea in me, Deus: et spiritum rectum innova in visceribus meis.

    A clean heart create for me, O God, and a steadfast spirit renew within me.

13. Redde mihi laetitiam salutaris tui: et spiritu
    principali confirma me.

    Give me back the joy of your salvation, and a
    willing spirit sustain in me.

15. Libera me de sanguinibus, Deus, Deus salutis
    meae: et exsultabit lingua mea justitiam tuam.

    Free me from blood guilt, O God, my saving God;
    then my tongue shall revel in your justice.

17. Quoniam si voluisses sacrificium, dedissem utique:
    holocaustis non delectaberis.

    For you are not pleased with sacrifices; should I
    offer a holocaust, you would not accept it.

19. Benigne fac, Domine, in bona voluntate tua Sion:
    ut aedificentur muri Jerusalem.

    Be bountiful, O Lord, to Sion in your kindness by
    rebuilding the walls of Jerusalem.

20. Tunc imponent super altare tuum vitulos.

    Then shall they offer up bullocks on your alter.

Corrections

Cor mundum (folio 8v-9)
m. 10, sop, ms has an A and no rest

De Lamentatione Jeremiae (Mata), folio 12v-13
This four-voice setting of the Lamentations of Jere-
miah was written for the first nocturn, first lesson,
of Good Friday matins as the title reads "feria 6 in
Parasceve." It must have been widely performed, for
it can be found also in the Carmen Codex (see preface
and page 161 of Bal y Gay's edition) without the Jod
setting. Mata's name does not appear in that manuscript, but by comparison with the 1717 choirbook iden-
tification was possible. His Passions according to

St. Matthew and St. John as well as still another copy
of these Lamentations, also without the Jod setting
have been preserved in the Mexico City Cathedral
archives choirbook Inventario: Departmento XXIX,
Oficina 71, Obra 17, which was copied in 1750 (Libro
polifónica I of the Spiess-Stanford catalogue).

Text

De Lamentatione Jeremiae Prophetae.

From the Lamentation of Jeremia the Prophet.

Heth. Cogitavit Dominus dissipare murum filiae Sion:
tetendit funiculum suum, et non avertit manum suam a
perditione: luxitque antemurale, et murus pariter dis-
sipatus est.

Heth. The Lord marked for destruction the wall of
daughter Sion: He stretched out the measuring line;
his hand brought ruin, yet he did not relent--he
brought grief on wall and rampart till both succumbed.

Teth. Defixae sunt in terra portae ejus: perdidit, et
contrivit vectes ejus: regem ejus et principes ejus in
Gentibus: non est lex, et prophetae ejus non invene-
runt visionem a Domino.

Teth. Sunk into the ground are her gates; he has
removed and broken her bars. Her king and her princes
are among the pagans; priestly instruction is wanting,
and her prophets have not received any vision from the
Lord.

Jod. Sederunt in terra, conticuerunt senes filiae
Sion: consperserunt cinere capita sua, accincti sunt
ciliciis, abjecerunt in terram capita sua virgines
Jerusalem.

Jod. On the ground in silence sit the old men of
daughter Sion; they strew dust on their heads and gird
themselves with sackcloth; the maidens of Jerusalem
bow their heads to the ground.

Caph. Defecerunt prae lacrimis oculi mei, conturbata sunt viscera mea: effusum est in terra jecur meum super contritione filiae populi mei, cum deficeret parvulus et lactens in plateis oppidi.

Caph. Worn out from weeping are my eyes, within me all is in ferment; my gall is poured out on the ground because of the downfall of the daughter of my people, as child and infant faint away in the open spaces of the town.

Jerusalem, Jerusalem, convertere ad Dominum Deum tuum.

Jerusalem, Jerusalem, return to the Lord your God.

Corrections

Teth (folio 15v-16)
m. 3, ten, ms has SSS

Defixae sunt
m. 29, tie has been added, ms has only a B

Defecerunt (folio 19v-20)
m. 12, ten, ms has M

De Lamentatione Jeremiae (Sumaya), folio 22v-23
This four-voice work has the title Sabbato Sancto in the manuscript and was written for the first nocturn, first lesson, Holy Saturday matins. The manuscript is decorated with beautiful drawings of the Hebrew letters Heth, Teth, and Jod (see facsimile).

Text

De Lamentatione Jeremiae Prophetae.

From the Lamentation of Jeremia the Prophet.

Heth. Misericordiae Domini quia non sumus consumpti: quia non defecerunt miserationes ejus.

Heth. The favors of the Lord are not exhausted, his mercies are not spent.

Heth. Novi diluculo, multa est fides tua.

Heth. They are renewed each morning, so great is his faithfulness.

Heth. Pars mea Dominus, dixit anima mea: propterea exspectabo eum.

Heth. My portion is the Lord, says my soul; therefore will I hope in him.

Teth. Bonus est Dominus sperantibus in eum, animae quaerenti illum.

Teth. Good is the Lord to one who waits for him, to the soul that seeks him.

Teth. Bonum est praestolari cum silentio salutare Dei.

Teth. It is good to hope in silence for the saving help of the Lord.

Teth. Bonum est viro, cum portaverit jugum ab adolescentia sua.

Teth. It is good for a man to bear the yoke from his youth.

Jod. Sedebit solitarius, et tacebit: quia levavit super se.

Jod. Let him sit alone and in silence, when it is laid upon him.

Jod. Ponet in pulvere os suum, si forte sit spes.

Jod. Let him put his mouth to the dust; there may yet be hope.

Jod. Dabit percutienti se maxillam, saturabitur oppro-
briis.

Jod. Let him offer his cheek to be struck, let him be
filled with disgrace.

Jerusalem, Jerusalem, convertere ad Dominum Deum tuum.

Jerusalem, Jerusalem, return to the Lord your God.

Corrections

Misericordia (folio 23v-24)
m. 3, alt, second note, ms has a C̄
m. 9, sop, third note, ms has S̲

Heth (folio 25v-26)
m. 5, ms has ⌐⌐.

Pars mea
m. 4, third note, ms has S̄
m. 8, second note, ms has a B̲

Teth (folio 27v-28)
m. 6, ba, ms has ⌐⌐. Parallel octaves between ten and
ba m. 5-6 in original

Teth (folio 28v-29)
m. 1, ten, ms has ⌐⌐

Bonum est viro
m. 5, sop, ms has O. (dot is a mistake)

Jod (folio 30v-31)
m. 4, sop, ms has ⌐⌐. Sometimes in ligatures of this
type the figures appear over the notes, possibly to
warn that the two notes have the value of a breve
each. One is reminded of Cerone's instructional use of
such figures in his El Melopeo y Maestro (Naples,
1613).

Jod (folio 31v-32)
m. 1, alt, ms has ⌐.
m. 1, ba, ms has ⌐⌐.

<u>Christus</u> <u>factus</u> <u>est</u> (Sumaya?), folio 33v-34
This is a four-part setting of the gradual for Maundy
Thursday Mass. Neither title nor composer is given in
the choirbook, but Sumaya's stylistic characteristics
are easily identifiable.

Text

Christus factus est pro nobis obediens usque ad mortem, mortem autem crucis.

Christ became obedient for us unto death, even to
death on a cross.

Propter quod et Deus exaltavit illum, et dedit illi
nomen, quo est super omne nomen.

Therefore, God also has exalted him and has given him
the name that is above every name.

Corrections

Propter quod (folio 34v-35)
m. 19, alt, second note, ms has <u>L</u>

<u>Miserere</u> <u>mei</u> <u>Deus</u> (Sumaya), folio 35v-36
This is another four-part setting of Psalm 50 with the
same text as Sumaya's "año 1717" setting, to which it
may have provided an alternate use on Maundy Thursday
or Holy Saturday.

Corrections

Miserere (folio 35v-36)
m. 4, ten, ms has dot after first note

Auditui meo (folio 38v-39)
m. 4, the parallel fifths between alt and sop are in
ms
m. 7, alt, last note, ms has a <u>G</u>
m. 11, sop, last note, ms has an <u>S</u>
m. 12, sop, second note, ms has an <u>M</u>

Quoniam si (folio 42v-43)
m. 2, sop, first two notes, ms has ·M M
m. 3, sop, first two notes, ms has M̄ M̄
m. 12, sop, third note, ms has an F̲

Benigne fac (folio 43v-44)
m. 2, ten, from second note ms has

m. 12, ba, from third note, ms has

Gloria
m. 6,7,8, ten, from the E̲, ms has

Alleluia: Dic nobis (López Capillas), folio 46v-47
Neither title nor composer is given here for this
Easter piece which was copied into the end of the manuscript by a different, unnamed scribe. It was identi-
fied, however, inasmuch as it appears also in the
cathedral choirbook Inventario: Departamento XXIX,
Oficina 71, Obra 25, where it is listed Sequentia, In
resurrectione Dom. ad IV et ad duo. It is the last
half of the text of the Easter sequence, Victimae
paschali laudes, so arranged as to emphasize and
repeat the interrogation of Mary Magdalene: "Speak,
Mary, declaring, what thou sawest wayfaring," with the
Alleluia used a refrain after each verse.

Text

Alleluia!
Dic nobis, Maria
Quid vidisti in via?

Alleluia!
Speak, Mary, declaring
What thou sawest, wayfaring.

Alleluia!
Sepulchrum Christi viventis,
et gloriam vidi, resurgentis.

Alleluia!
The tomb of Christ, who is living,
The glory of Jesus' resurrection.

Alleluia!
Dic nobis, Maria
Quid vidisti in via?

Alleluia!
Speak, Mary, declaring
What thou sawest, wayfaring.

Alleluia!
Angelicos testes,
sudarium, et vestes.

Alleluia!
Bright angels attesting,
The shroud and napkin resting.

Alleluia!
Dic nobis, Maria
Quid vidisti in via?

Alleluia!
Speak, Mary, declaring
What thou sawest, wayfaring.

Alleluia!
Surrexit Christus, spes mea:
praecedet vos in Galilaeam.

Alleluia!
Yea Christ, my hope is arisen:
To Galilee he goes before you.

Alleluia!
Dic nobis, Maria
Quid vidisti in via?

Alleluia!
Speak, Mary, declaring
What thou sawest, wayfaring.

Alleluia!
Scimus Christum surrexisse
a mortuis vere:

tu nobis, victor Rex miserere.
Amen. Alleluia.

Alleluia!
Christ indeed from
death is risen,
our new life obtaining.
Have mercy, victor King,
ever reigning.
Amen. Alleluia!

Corrections

Alleluia (folio 46v-47)
m. 24, one might add here "da capo al segno $\int$, e poi il segiente." The Alleluia should be repeated.

m. 27, sop, last note lacking in ms

m. 52, alt and ba, the word vos is the original text, and this has not been corrected to suos.

Christum Regem (Sumaya), folio 0v-1
This four-voice setting of the invitatory for matins of the feast of Corpus Christi is short and simple, which would permit its performance in connection with Venite, exsultemus Domino (Psalm 94). The piece consists of (a) Christum regem of sixteen measures and (b) Qui se manducantibus of eight measures. In actual performance (a) is repeated and then the first verse of Psalm 94 follows. This is followed by (a), second verse of the psalm, (b), third verse, (a), fourth verse (b), fifth verse, (a), the Gloria Patri, (b), (a), (b) (see Liber Usualis, p. 918).

Text

Christum Regem adoremus, dominantem gentibus: Qui se manducantibus dat Spiritus pinquedinem.

Let us adore Christ the King, who rules the nations: who gives richness of spirit to those who eat him.

<u>Sacris solemnis</u> (Sumaya?), folio 2v-3
This is the hymn for <u>Corpus Christi</u> matins which follows the <u>Christum Regem</u> and <u>Venite, exsultemus</u>. It is
a four-part chordal setting of verses one, five and
seven of the hymn. Only the text for the first verse
has been provided in the score. See below for the
texts for verses five and seven. Although Sumaya's
name does not appear above this piece, there is no
doubt that he is the composer due to the connection
between this work and the previous one.

Text

Sacris solemniis juncta sint gaudia,
Et ex praecordiis sonent praeconia:
Recedant vetera, nova sint omnia;
Corda, voces et opera.

At this our solemn feast,
Let holy joys abound,
And from the inmost breast
Let songs of praise resound;
Let ancient rites depart,
And all be new around,
In ev'ry act, and voice, and heart.

Sic sacrificium istud instituit,
Cujus officium
committi voluit Solis presbyteris,
quibus sic congruit,
Ut sumant, et dent ceteris.

So he this Sacrifice
To institute did will,
And charged his priests alone
That office to fulfill:
In them he did confide:
To whom pertaineth still
To take, and to the rest divide.

Te trina Deitas unaque poscimus,
Sic nos tu visita,
sicut te colimus:

Per tuas semitas duc nos quo tendimus,
Ad lucem quam inhabitas. Amen.

Thee therefore we implore,
O Godhead, One in Three,
So mayst thou visit us
As we now worship thee;
And lead us on thy way,
That we at last may see
The light wherein thou dwellest aye. Amen.

Magnificat primi toni (Sumaya), folio 4v-5
In this, the first of three four-part settings of the odd-numbered verses for vespers, one notes the use of the chant patterns as cantus in the tenor of Deposuit and in the soprano in the Gloria. Each of these Magnificats has the opening intonation in the choirbook.

Text

1. Magnificat anima mea Dominum.

   My soul magnifies the Lord.

3. Quia respexit humilitatem ancillae suae; ecce enim ex hoc beatam me dicent omnes generationes.

   Because he has regarded the lowliness of his handmaid; for, behold, henceforth all generations shall call me blessed.

5. Et misericordia ejus a progenie in progenies timentibus eum.

   And his mercy is from generation to generation on those who fear him.

7. Deposuit potentes de sede, et exaltavit humiles.

   He has put down the mighty from their thrones, and has exalted the lowly.

9. Suscepit Israel puerum suum, recordatus misericordiae suae.

He has given help to Israel, his servant, mindful
of his mercy.

11. Gloria Patri, et Filio, et Spiritui Sancto.

Glory be to the Father, and to the Son, and to the
Holy Ghost.

Corrections

Suscepit (folio 8v-9)
In sop, alt, and ten Israel is spelled Isrrael, possibly reflecting an Hispanicized pronunciation of a
rolled R after an S sung at the time.
m. 13, ba, third note, ms has M

Magnificat secundi toni (Sumaya), folio 10v-11
The chant cantus appears in the tenor of the Gloria.
All three magnificats in this book use a three-part
setting of the Misericordia with the soprano tacet.

Corrections

Suscepit (folio 14v-15)
In all parts ms spells Israel as Isrrael.

Magnificat tertii toni (Sumaya), folio 16v-17
The chant appears in the tenor of the Quia respexit.
At folio 21v-22 one reads above the tenor of the
Gloria "Altus in Diathessaron superiore, Bassus in
sub-Diapente, Unitas in trinitare." This three-in-one
canon leaves the soprano free to add a decorative line
above the other parts.

Corrections

Suscepit (folio 20v-21)
Israel is spelled Isrrael in all parts in ms.

O sacrum convivium (Antonio Salazar), folio 22v-23
This is a setting for two four-part choirs of the antiphon at Magnificat (vespers) for the feast of Corpus
Christi. The absence of text for the bass parts in the
original strongly indicates the use of instruments.
This piece reflects the Baroque style not present in
other works of the collection and exemplifies the
polychoric tradition flourishing in the Cathedrals of
Mexico City and Puebla. On page 51 of the previously
cited article by Anthony M. Cummings, one reads of
references from the Diarii sistini for 1594 relating
motets to liturgical contexts at the end of the Mass.
There is clear evidence here that O Sacrum Convivium
was so used as well as after Communion. Cummings
points out that according to Josef Andreas Jungman
this text was traditionally sung at some ecclesias-
tical centers after the silent prayer that follows
Communion.

Text

O sacrum convivium! in quo Christus sumitur: recolitur
memoria passionis ejus: mens impletur gratia; et
futurae gloriae nobis pignus datur.

O sacred Banquet, wherein Christ is received, the memo-
rial of his passion is celebrated, the mind is filled
with grace, and a pledge of future glory is given to
us.

Confitebor tibi Domine (Sumaya), folio 26v-27
This four-part setting of the odd-numbered verses of
Psalm 137 adds a second soprano part for the Gloria
Patri. The psalm tone is moved from the soprano for
the first verse to the tenor, alto, and bass in suc-
ceeding verses, with a return to the first soprano for
the Gloria. The psalm was used at Thursday vespers and
in the Office for the Dead.

1. Confitebor tibi Domine in toto corde meo: quoniam
   audisti verba oris mei.

I will give thanks to you, O Lord, with all my heart, for you have heard the words of my mouth.

3. Super misericordia tua et veritate tua: quoniam magnificasti super omne, nomen sanctum tuum.

   Because of your kindness and your truth; for you have made great above all things your name and your promise.

5. Confiteantur tibi Domine omnes reges terrae: quia audierunt omnia verba oris tui.

   All the kings of the earth shall give thanks to you, O Lord, when they hear the words of your mouth.

7. Quoniam excelsus Dominus, et humilia respicit: et alta a longe cognoscit.

   The Lord is exalted, yet the lowly he sees, and the proud he knows from afar.

9. Dominus retribuet pro me: Domine, misericordia tua in saeculum: opera manuum tuarum ne despicias.

   The Lord will complete what he has done for me; your kindness, O Lord, endures forever; forsake not the work of your hands.

10. Gloria Patri, et Filio, et Spiritui Sancto.

    Glory be to the Father, and to the Son, and to the Holy Ghost. Amen.

Credidi propter quod (Sumaya), folio 32v-33
In a manner similar to Psalm 137, this four-part setting of the odd-numbered verses of Psalm 115 adds a second soprano for the Gloria Patri. Here, however, Sumaya writes a double canon (as in the Gloria Patri of Magnificat III), but he gives the chant melody to the second soprano and a free part to the first soprano. With the tenor beginning, the bass enters at

a fifth below and then the alto follows at a fourth above. Throughout the psalm the chant tone is passed around, first to the tenor, and then in successive verses to the alto, bass, and finally soprano before the Gloria Patri. Sung at Monday vespers, the psalm was also used at Maundy Thursday vespers.

Text

1. Credidi, propter quod locutus sum: ego autem humiliatus sum nimis.

   I believed, even when I said, "I am greatly afflicted."

3. Quid retribuam Domino, pro omnibus quae retribuit mihi?

   How shall I make a return to the Lord for all the good he has done for me?

5. Vota mea Domino reddam coram omni populo ejus: pretiosa in conspectu Domini mors sanctorum ejua.

   My vows to the Lord I will pay in the presence of all his people.

7. Dirupisti vincula mea: tibi sacrificabo hostiam laudis, et nomen Domini invocabo.

   O Lord, I am your servant; I am your servant, the son of your handmaid; you have loosed my bonds.

9. Gloria Patri, et Filio, et Spirituai Sancto.

   Glory be to the father, and to the Son, and to the Holy Ghost.

Corrections

Gloria (folio 36v-37)
m. 21, alt, ms has word et repeated on second note.

ENDNOTES

1. The numberings of the manuscripts used in this edition are those placed on the books by the Mexican government, presumably in the late 1920s. Although these numbers have no particular significance, they are used throughout this study because they are still on the books. For reference, however, the numbers assigned these choirbooks by Lincoln Spiess and Thomas Stanford in An Introduction to Certain Mexican Musical Archives are as follows: Departamento XXIX, Oficina 71, Obra 14, is Libro polifónico III, Catedral Metropolitana de México. Departamento XXIX, Oficina 71, Obra 24, is Libro polifónico II, Museo del Virreinato, Tepotzotlán.

2. Lester D. Brothers, "A New-World Hexachord Mass by Francisco López Capillas," Yearbook for Inter-American Musical Research 9(1973), 5.

3. Jo Ann Smith has undertaken a full study of the works of López Capillas for her University of Southern California Ph.D. dissertation. The title "The Masses and Magnificats of Francisco López y Capillas in Ms. 2428, Biblioteca Nacional, Madrid," is registered in Cecil Adkins and Alis Dichinson, eds., "Supplement (1973) to Doctoral Dissertations in Musicology," Journal of the American Musicology Society, p. 448. Roberto Rivera y Rivera in Mexico City is also preparing an edition of the Magnificats of López y Capillas.

4. Music in the Baroque Era (New York: Norton, 1947), p. 3.

5. Ibid.

6. Thomas Gage's Travels in the New World, ed. J. E. S. Thompson (Norman: Univ. of Oklahoma Press, 1958), p. 72.

7. The information contained in this chapter comes largely from the Actas Capitulares of the Mexico City Cathedral. I am grateful to Robert Stevenson for sharing his notes, which were painstakingly prepared from

these Actas from the Cathedral's archives, to which
I have not had access. Stevenson's "Mexico City
Cathedral Music: 1600-1750," The Americas 21 (Oct.
1964) deals more extensively with this subject.
References to specific Actas are meticulously cited in
this article and will not be repeated here.

8. These volumes, which have been in the Newberry
Library for over eighty years, came to light in the
late 1960s. Eliyahu Schleifer, as a graduate student
at the University of Chicago, prepared a detailed
study of the manuscripts for his doctoral dissertation.

9. Carol Tarrh, as a graduate student at Southern
Illinois University, Carbondale, treated these psalms
and other works of Ximeno in her master's degree the-
sis in 1969.

10. Robert Stevenson, who recently discovered the will
of López Capillas, has supplied the most up-to-date
information about his provenance and death date.

Part One

Cathedral *Inventario:*
Departmento XXIX, Oficina 71, Obra 14

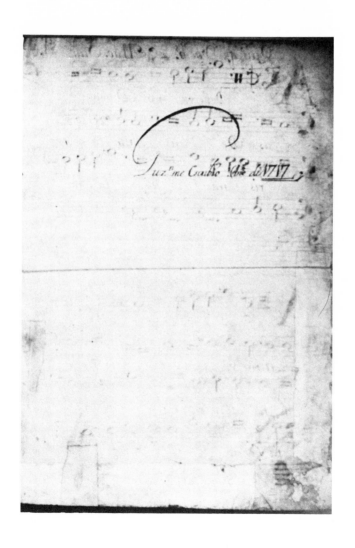

Adjuva nos Deus

Manuel de Sumaya

1

Adjuva nos Deus

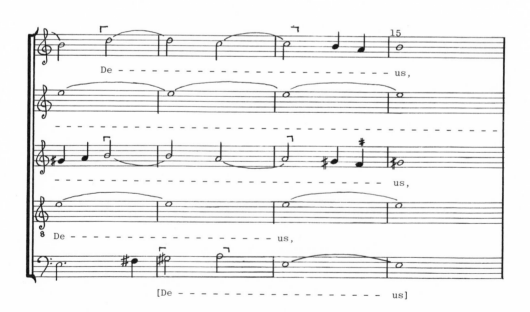

2

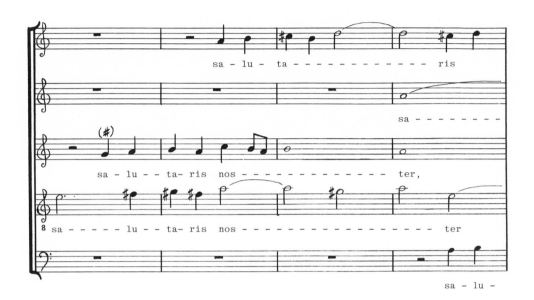

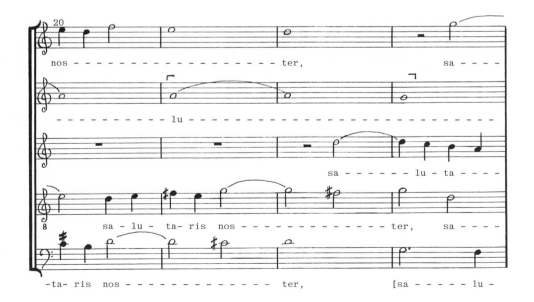

3

Adjuva nos Deus

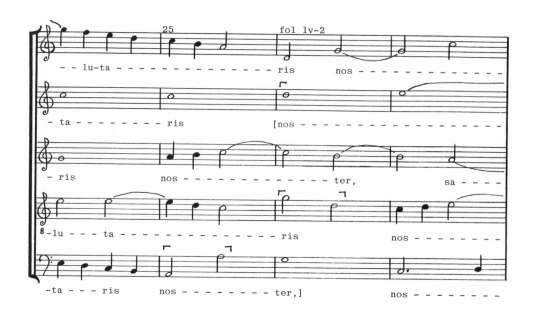

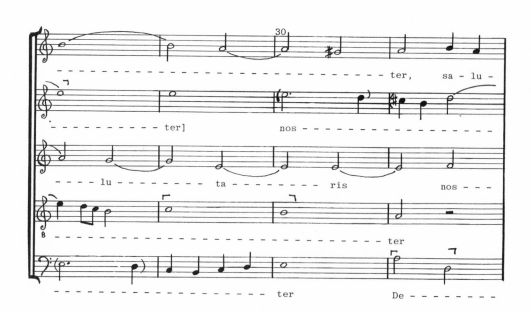

4

Manuel de Sumaya

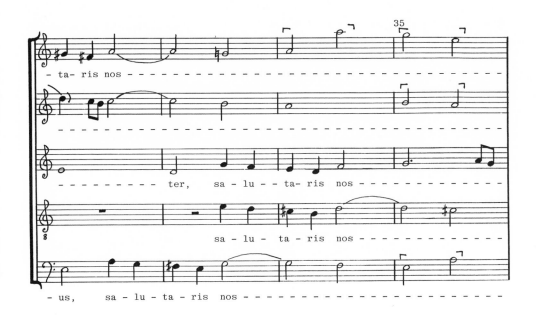

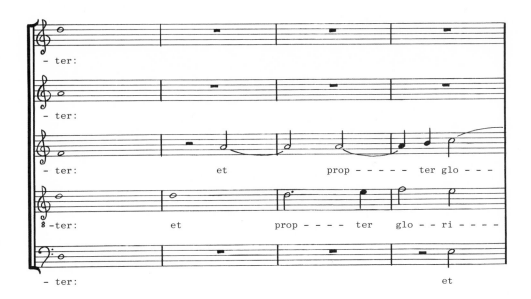

Adjuva nos Deus

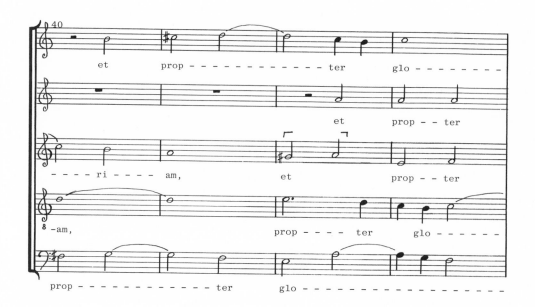

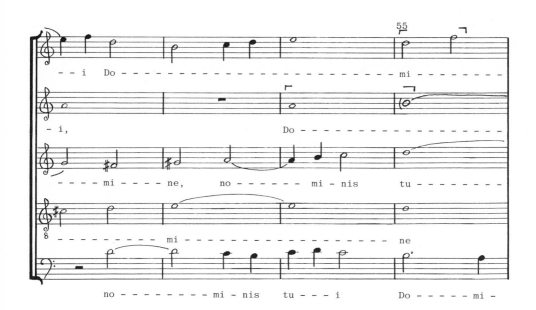

Adjuva nos Deus

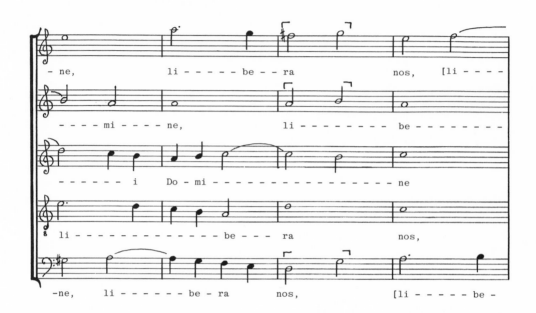

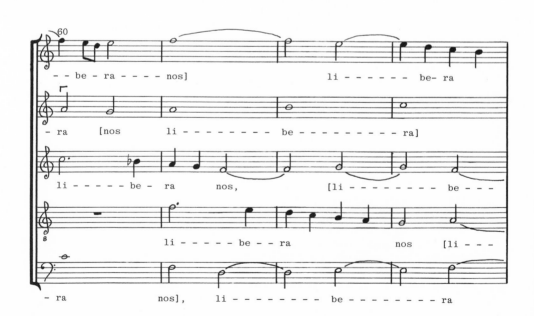

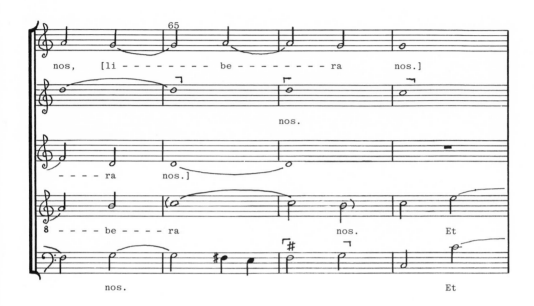

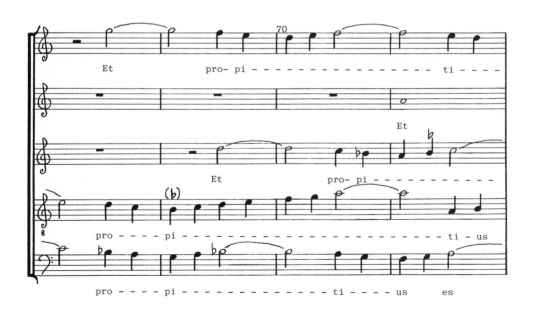

Adjuva nos Deus

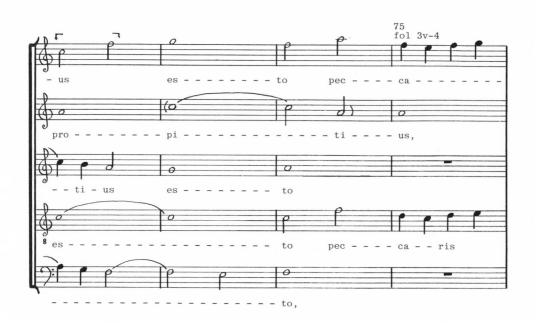

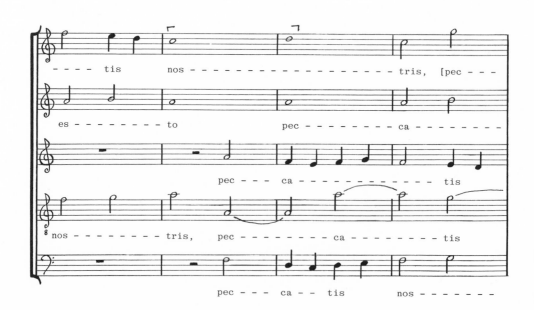

10

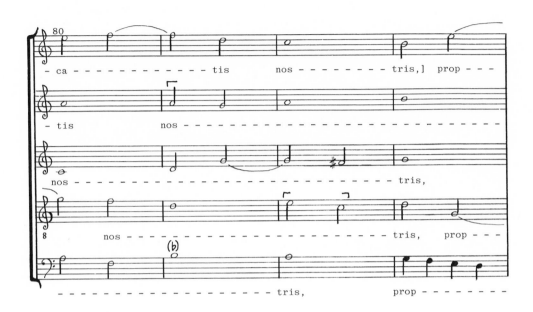

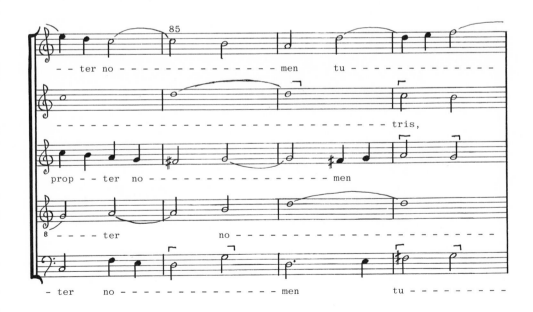

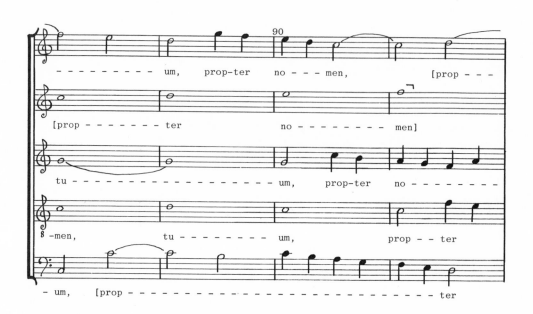

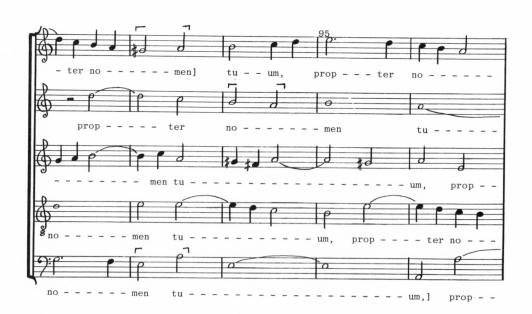

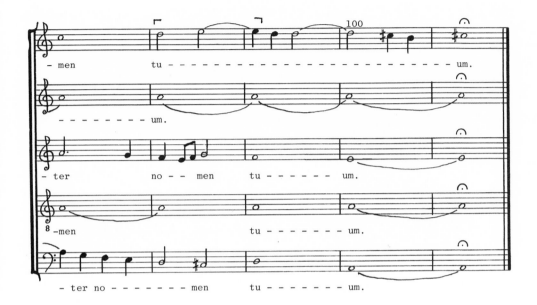

Miserere (1717)

Manuel de Sumaya

Miserere

Miserere

Miserere

Miserere

24

Miserere

De Lamentatione Jeremiae Feria sexta

Antonio Rodríguez de Mata

Lamentatione Jeremiae, Feria sexta

31

Lamentatione Jeremiae, Feria sexta

37

Lamentatione Jeremiae, Feria sexta

39

Caph.

De Lamantatione Jeremiae, Sabbato Sancto

Manuel de Sumaya

Manuel de Sumaya

51

Lamentatione Jeremiae, Sabbato Sancto

Manuel de Sumaya

Lamentatione Jeremiae, Sabbato Sancto

55

Lamentatione Jeremiae, Sabbato Sancto

Lamentatione Jeremiae, Sabbato Sancto

61

62

63

Lamentatione Jeremiae, Sabbato Sancto

65

Christus factus est

(Manuel de Sumaya)

Christus factus est

68

(Manuel de Sumaya)

fol 34v-35

69

Christus factus est

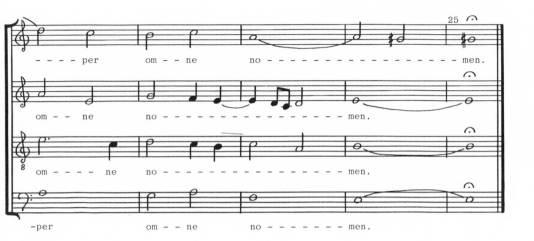

Miserere

Manuel de Sumaya

Miserere

74

Miserere

76

Miserere

Miserere

Miserere

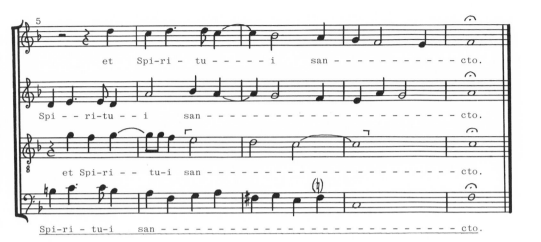

Alleluia! Dic nobis Maria

Francisco López Capillas

Francisco López Capillas

87

Alleluia! Dic nobis Maria

Alleluia! Dic nobis Maria

Alleluia! Dic nobis Maria

Part Two

Cathedral *Inventario:*
Departmento XXIX, Oficina 71, Obra 24

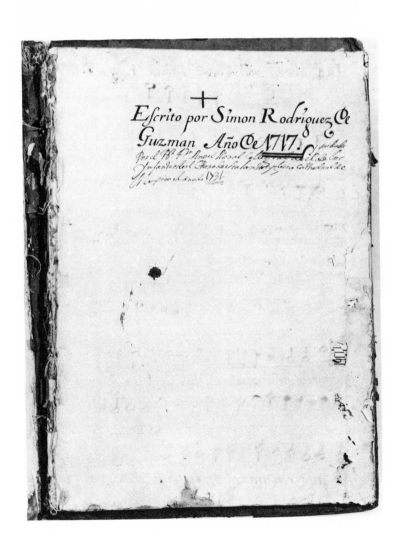

Christum Regem

Manuel de Sumaya

Manuel de Sumaya

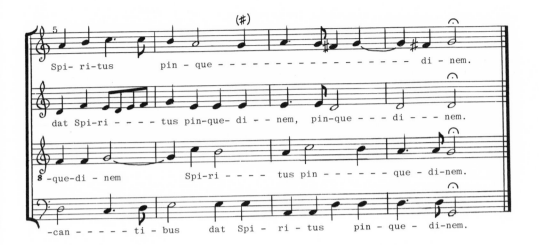

Sacris Solemnis

Manuel de Sumaya

101

Sacris Solemnis

Magnificat primi toni

Manuel de Sumaya

105

Magnificat primi toni

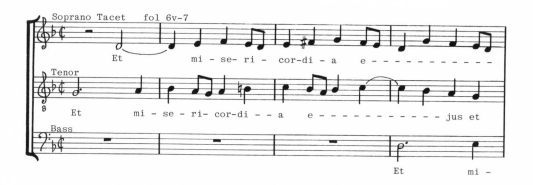

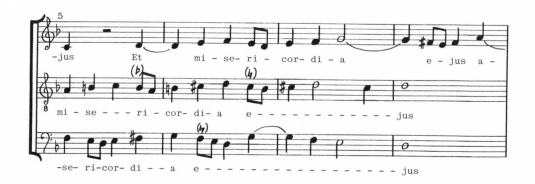

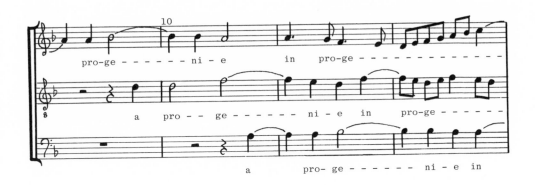

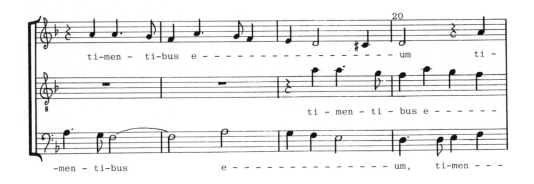

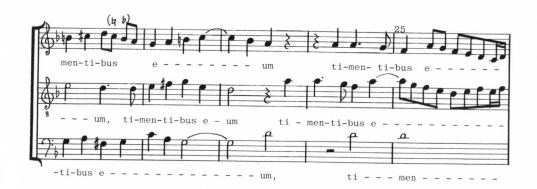

109

Magnificat primi toni

110

111

Magnificat primi toni

Manuel de Sumaya

113

Magnificat segundi toni

Manuel de Sumaya

Magnificat secundi toni

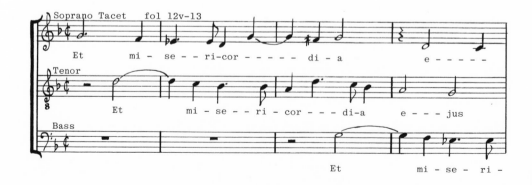

Manuel de Sumaya

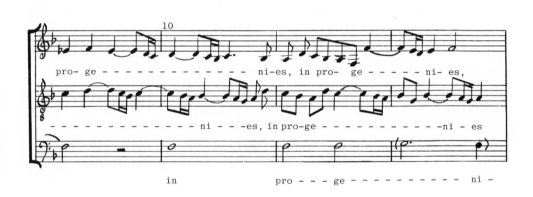

Magnificat secundi toni

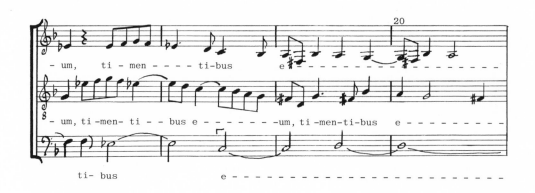

119

Magnificat secundi toni

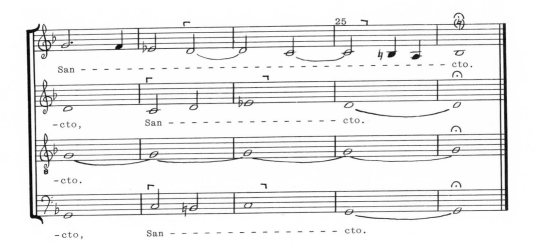

San - cto.

-cto,   San - - - - - - - - - - - - cto.

-cto.

-cto,   San - - - - - - - - - - - - - cto.

Magnificat tertii toni

Manuel de Sumaya

Manuel de Sumaya

125

Magnificat tertii toni

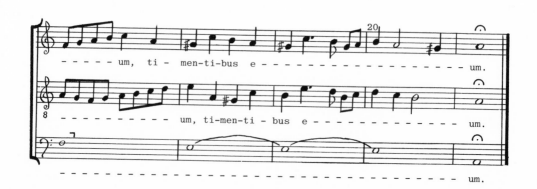

Magnificat tertii toni

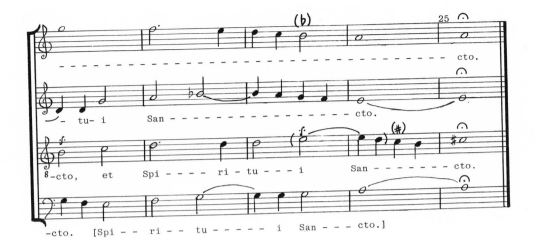

O Sacrum Convivium

Antonio de Salazar

Antonio de Salazar

fol 23v-24

Antonio de Salazar

Antonio de Salazar

Antonio de Salazar

Confitebor tibi Domine: Psalmus 137

Manuel de Sumaya

Confitebor titi Domine

146

147

Confitebor titi Domine

148

Confitebor titi Domine

151

Confitebor titi Domine

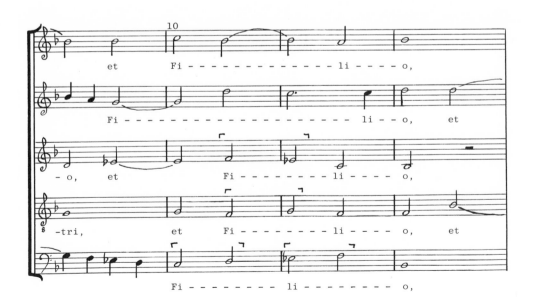

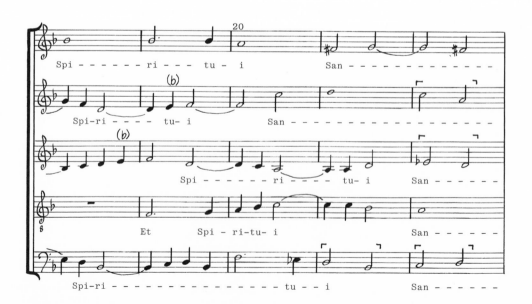

Credidi propter quod locutus sum: Psalmus 115

Manuel de Sumaya

157

Credidi propter quod locutus sum

158

Credidi propter quod locutus sum

Manuel de Sumaya

161

Credidi propter quod locutus sum

Credidi propter quod locutus sum